Navigating the Digital Gold Rush:

A Guide to Making Money in the Digital Age

Foliage Series

THIS BOOK

In "Navigating the Digital Gold Rush," readers are taken on a journey through the vast landscape of the digital age, exploring the myriad opportunities for success in an ever-evolving digital economy. This comprehensive guide is designed to empower individuals with the knowledge, strategies, and resources needed to thrive in the digital era.

From building a strong online presence and monetizing skills and expertise to investing in digital assets and harnessing the power of e-commerce, each chapter provides practical insights, actionable advice, and real-world examples to help readers navigate the complexities of the digital landscape with confidence.

Through in-depth discussions on topics such as passive income generation, gig economy opportunities, and staying ahead of technological advancements, readers gain a deeper understanding of how to leverage the digital revolution to achieve financial freedom, career satisfaction, and personal fulfillment.

Whether you're an aspiring entrepreneur, freelancer, investor, or digital enthusiast, "Navigating the Digital Gold Rush" serves as your indispensable roadmap to success in the digital age, equipping you with the tools and strategies needed to thrive amidst uncertainty and seize the boundless opportunity of digital gold rush.

Product of Foliage Series Books

TABLE OF CONTENT

THIS BOOK 2

CHAPTER 1

Building Your Online Presence 8

    Establishing your brand identity 8

    Creating a compelling digital presence 9

    Leveraging social media platforms effectively 10

CHAPTER 2

Monetizing Your Skills and Expertise. 12

    Identifying your strengths and passions 12

    Exploring freelance opportunities and online marketplaces 13

    Creating and selling digital products or services ... 13

    Building Your Personal Brand 14

    Scaling Your Business 15

CHAPTER 3

Investing in Digital Assets 16

    Understanding cryptocurrency and blockchain technology 16

    Exploring investment opportunities in digital currencies 17

    Diversifying your portfolio with digital assets 17

Risk Management and Security 18

CHAPTER 4
Harnessing the Power of E-commerce 20
Setting up an online store 20
Utilizing dropshipping and print-on-demand services 21
Optimizing sales through effective marketing strategies 22

CHAPTER 5
Embracing the Gig Economy 24
Exploring gig platforms and job opportunities 24
Maximizing earnings through multiple gigs and flexible work arrangements 25
Managing finances and planning for long-term sustainability 26
Embracing the Future of Work 27

CHAPTER 6
Creating Passive Income Streams. 29
Creating Passive Income Streams 29
Investing in affiliate marketing and sponsored content 30
Exploring opportunities in digital real estate and royalties 30

Passive Investing 31
Nurturing and Scaling Passive Income Streams ... 32

CHAPTER 7
Navigating Challenges and Staying Ahead. 34
Adapting to technological advancements and market trends 34
Overcoming obstacles and setbacks in the digital landscape 35
Continuing education and lifelong learning for sustained success 36
Future-proofing Your Career or Business 37

Conclusion
Embracing the limitless possibilities of the digital age 39
Taking action and seizing opportunities for financial growth 39
Empowering yourself to thrive in the ever-evolving digital economy 40

CHAPTER 1

Building Your Online Presence

Establishing your brand identity

Define your niche: Identify your unique skills, expertise, and passions.

Craft your brand story: Communicate your values, mission, and vision to resonate with your target audience.

Design a memorable brand identity: Create a logo, choose a color palette, and develop a consistent visual style across all platforms.

Choose your brand voice: Determine the tone and language that best represents your brand personality.

Conduct market research: Understand your target audience's preferences, needs, and pain points to tailor your brand message effectively.

Creating a compelling digital presence

Build a professional website: Invest in a user-friendly website with clear navigation, engaging content, and mobile responsiveness.

Optimize for search engines (SEO): Implement SEO strategies to improve your website's visibility and rank higher in search engine results.

Develop a content strategy: Produce high-quality, relevant content to attract and engage your audience. Consider blogging, videos, podcasts, or infographics.

Leverage email marketing: Build an email list and send regular newsletters or promotional offers to nurture relationships with your audience.

Utilize multimedia content: Incorporate images, videos, and interactive elements to enhance user experience and drive engagement.

Leveraging social media platforms effectively

Choose the right platforms: Identify the social media channels where your target audience is most active and focus your efforts there.

Create engaging content: Develop a content calendar and share valuable, shareable content consistently to build a loyal following.

Engage with your audience: Respond to comments, messages, and mentions promptly to foster meaningful connections and community engagement.

Utilize social media advertising: Experiment with paid advertising options on platforms like Facebook, Instagram, and LinkedIn to expand your reach and drive conversions.

Analyze and optimize: Monitor your social media metrics and use analytics tools to track performance, identify trends, and adjust your strategy accordingly for continuous improvement.

By focusing on building a strong online presence, individuals and businesses can establish credibility, expand their reach, and ultimately increase their opportunities for success in the digital age.

CHAPTER 2

Monetizing Your Skills and Expertise.

Identifying your strengths and passions

Self-assessment: Reflect on your skills, knowledge, and experiences to identify your areas of expertise and passion.

Market research: Evaluate the demand for your skills in the digital marketplace and identify potential niches or industries where you can offer value.

Skill development: Invest in continuous learning and skill development to stay relevant and competitive in your chosen field.

Exploring freelance opportunities and online marketplaces

Freelancing platforms: Sign up on websites such as Upwork, Freelancer, or Fiverr to offer your services to a global audience.

Specialized marketplaces: Explore niche platforms tailored to your skills, such as 99designs for graphic designers or Toptal for freelance developers.

Networking: Leverage your professional network and online communities to find freelance opportunities and referrals.

Creating and selling digital products or services

Digital products: Develop digital products such as e-books, online courses, templates, or software tools based on your expertise and knowledge.

E-commerce platforms: Utilize platforms like Shopify, Etsy, or Gumroad to sell your digital products directly to consumers.

Subscription models: Offer subscription-based services, such as membership sites or monthly coaching programs, to generate recurring revenue from your expertise.

Building Your Personal Brand

Content creation: Establish yourself as an authority in your niche by creating valuable content through blogging, podcasting, or video creation.

Thought leadership: Share insights, tips, and industry trends on social media, forums, and professional networks to showcase your expertise and attract potential clients.

Testimonials and case studies: Collect testimonials and case studies from satisfied clients to build credibility and trust with prospective customers.

Scaling Your Business

Outsourcing and delegation: Delegate non-core tasks or projects to freelancers or virtual assistants to focus on high-value activities and scale your business efficiently.

Automation: Implement tools and systems to automate repetitive tasks, streamline processes, and optimize productivity.

Diversification: Explore opportunities to expand your revenue streams by offering new services, products, or premium packages to meet the evolving needs of your audience.

By leveraging your skills and expertise effectively, you can create multiple streams of income, build a sustainable business, and achieve financial success in the digital age.

CHAPTER 3

Investing in Digital Assets

Understanding cryptocurrency and blockchain technology

Cryptocurrency basics: Learn about digital currencies like Bitcoin, Ethereum, and other altcoins, including their underlying technology, features, and use cases.

Blockchain fundamentals: Understand the decentralized ledger technology that powers cryptocurrencies, its principles of transparency, immutability, and security.

Risks and rewards: Educate yourself about the risks associated with investing in cryptocurrencies, including market volatility, regulatory uncertainty, and security threats, balanced with the potential rewards of high returns and diversification.

Exploring investment opportunities in digital currencies

Investment strategies: Research and develop a clear investment strategy based on your risk tolerance, investment goals, and time horizon, whether it's long-term holding, swing trading, or day trading.

Portfolio diversification: Diversify your cryptocurrency portfolio across different assets, including established cryptocurrencies, promising altcoins, and stablecoins, to mitigate risk and maximize potential returns.

Due diligence: Conduct thorough research and analysis before investing in any cryptocurrency, including evaluating the project's team, technology, community, and market dynamics.

Diversifying your portfolio with digital assets

Non-fungible tokens (NFTs): Explore the emerging market of digital collectibles, artwork, and unique assets represented as NFTs on blockchain platforms like Ethereum, and consider investing in high-quality NFTs with long-term value potential.

Decentralized finance (DeFi): Participate in decentralized finance platforms and protocols that enable peer-to-peer lending, borrowing, trading, and yield farming, leveraging smart contracts and blockchain technology to democratize and innovate traditional financial services.

Digital real estate: Invest in virtual real estate assets within blockchain-based virtual worlds or metaverse platforms, where users can buy, sell, and monetize digital land, properties, and virtual assets.

Risk Management and Security

Secure storage: Safeguard your digital assets by storing them in secure hardware wallets, cold storage solutions, or reputable cryptocurrency exchanges with strong security measures, such as multi-factor authentication and insurance coverage.

Risk assessment: Assess and manage the risks associated with investing in digital assets, including market volatility, technological vulnerabilities, regulatory changes, and potential scams or fraud.

Stay informed: Stay updated on the latest developments, news, and trends in the cryptocurrency and digital asset markets through reputable sources, community forums, and industry events to make informed investment decisions.

By understanding the opportunities and risks associated with investing in digital assets, individuals can diversify their investment portfolios, hedge against traditional market risks, and potentially generate significant returns in the digital age.

CHAPTER 4

Harnessing the Power of E-commerce

Setting up an online store

Choose an e-commerce platform: Select a suitable e-commerce platform based on your business needs, budget, and technical expertise, such as Shopify, WooCommerce, Magento, or BigCommerce.

Designing your store: Customize your online store's layout, theme, and branding elements to create a visually appealing and user-friendly shopping experience for customers.

Product listings: Create detailed product listings with high-quality images, descriptive titles, and compelling descriptions to showcase your products effectively and entice customers to make a purchase.

Payment gateways: Integrate secure payment gateways to accept various payment methods, including credit cards, digital wallets, and alternative payment options, to facilitate smooth transactions for customers.

Shipping and fulfillment: Set up shipping options, rates, and fulfillment processes to ensure timely delivery of orders and provide transparent shipping information to customers.

Utilizing dropshipping and print-on-demand services

Dropshipping basics: Partner with dropshipping suppliers or wholesalers to list and sell their products on your online store without holding inventory, handling fulfillment, or managing shipping logistics.

Print-on-demand services: Collaborate with print-on-demand providers to offer customized merchandise, such as apparel, accessories, or home decor, featuring your designs or artwork, with products manufactured and shipped on-demand as orders are received.

Product selection: Curate a diverse range of dropshipped or print-on-demand products that align with your target audience's interests, preferences, and purchasing behaviors to maximize sales potential.

Optimizing sales through effective marketing strategies

Search engine optimization (SEO): Optimize your e-commerce website for search engines by incorporating relevant keywords, optimizing product pages, and building high-quality backlinks to improve organic visibility and drive targeted traffic.

Content marketing: Create valuable, informative content, such as blog posts, product guides, or tutorials, to attract and engage potential customers, establish credibility, and drive organic traffic to your online store.

Social media marketing: Leverage social media platforms, such as Facebook, Instagram, Pinterest, and TikTok, to showcase your products, engage with your audience, and drive traffic and sales through targeted advertising, influencer partnerships, and user-generated content.

Email marketing: Build an email list of subscribers and send personalized email campaigns, newsletters, and promotional offers to nurture relationships with customers, encourage repeat purchases, and drive revenue growth.

Paid advertising: Invest in paid advertising channels, such as Google Ads, Facebook Ads, or Instagram Ads, to reach a broader audience, increase brand visibility, and drive targeted traffic to your e-commerce store through targeted ad campaigns and retargeting strategies.

By harnessing the power of e-commerce, individuals and businesses can establish scalable online storefronts, expand their reach to global markets, and capitalize on the growing trend of online shopping to drive sales and revenue growth in the digital age.

CHAPTER 5

Embracing the Gig Economy

Exploring gig platforms and job opportunities

Gig economy overview: Understand the concept of the gig economy, where individuals work on a freelance, temporary, or contract basis, often through online platforms, to provide services or complete tasks for clients or companies.

Popular gig platforms: Explore leading gig economy platforms, such as Upwork, Freelancer, TaskRabbit, Uber, Lyft, Airbnb, and DoorDash, that connect freelancers with clients or customers seeking various services, from writing and design to transportation and delivery.

Job opportunities: Browse and apply for gig opportunities across a wide range of industries and skill sets, including graphic design, writing, programming, digital marketing, virtual assistance, ridesharing, food delivery, and home services.

Maximizing earnings through multiple gigs and flexible work arrangements

Portfolio career: Build a portfolio of multiple gigs or side hustles to diversify income streams, reduce dependency on any single source of income, and maximize earning potential.

Flexible work schedules: Take advantage of the flexibility offered by gig work to create a customized work schedule that fits your lifestyle, preferences, and commitments, whether it's full-time, part-time, or occasional gigs.

Skill development: Continuously invest in upgrading and expanding your skills, expertise, and capabilities to qualify for higher-paying gigs, attract more clients, and stay competitive in the gig economy.

Managing finances and planning for long-term sustainability

Budgeting and financial planning: Develop a budgeting strategy to manage income and expenses effectively, prioritize savings and investments, and plan for short-term and long-term financial goals, such as retirement or emergency funds.

Income stability: Build a financial safety net by diversifying income sources, maintaining multiple gigs or clients, and creating passive income streams to mitigate the risks of income fluctuations and economic uncertainties.

Retirement planning: Take proactive steps to plan for retirement by contributing to retirement accounts, such as IRAs or 401(k)s, and exploring alternative retirement savings options, such as solo 401(k)s or SEP IRAs, tailored to gig workers and self-employed individuals.

Embracing the Future of Work

Remote work opportunities: Embrace remote work opportunities offered by gig platforms and companies to work from anywhere with an internet connection, enjoy location independence, and achieve a better work-life balance.

Gig economy trends: Stay informed about emerging trends and innovations in the gig economy, such as the rise of gig marketplaces, the gigification of traditional industries, and the adoption of technology-driven gig platforms and tools.

Professional networking: Build and nurture professional relationships with clients, peers, and industry professionals within the gig economy community through networking events, online forums, and social media platforms to access opportunities, share insights, and collaborate on projects.

By embracing the gig economy, individuals can leverage their skills, flexibility, and entrepreneurial spirit to create fulfilling and sustainable careers, achieve financial independence, and thrive in the evolving landscape of work in the digital age.

CHAPTER 6

Creating Passive Income Streams.

Creating Passive Income Streams

1. Building and monetizing a blog or YouTube channel

Content creation: Develop high-quality and valuable content around a specific niche or topic that appeals to your target audience's interests, needs, and pain points.

Audience engagement: Build a loyal audience by engaging with your viewers or readers through comments, social media, and email newsletters, and encouraging interaction and feedback.

Monetization strategies: Explore various monetization methods, such as display advertising, affiliate marketing, sponsored content, merchandise sales, memberships, or premium subscriptions, to generate passive income from your blog or YouTube channel.

Investing in affiliate marketing and sponsored content

Affiliate marketing basics: Partner with affiliate programs and promote products or services through unique affiliate links embedded in your content, earning commissions for referred sales or leads.

Sponsored content opportunities: Collaborate with brands, businesses, or advertisers to create sponsored content, such as product reviews, sponsored posts, or sponsored videos, in exchange for compensation or products/services.

Exploring opportunities in digital real estate and royalties

Digital real estate investments: Invest in digital assets, such as domain names, websites, apps, or social media accounts, with potential for appreciation or passive income through advertising revenue, affiliate partnerships, or resale.

Royalties and licensing: Create and monetize digital assets, such as e-books, music, photos, videos, or software, by licensing them for use or distribution through platforms, marketplaces, or royalty-based agreements.

Passive Investing

Dividend-paying stocks: Invest in dividend-paying stocks or dividend-focused exchange-traded funds (ETFs) to earn passive income through regular dividend distributions.

Real estate investment trusts (REITs): Allocate funds to REITs, which invest in income-generating real estate properties, to earn passive income from rental income and property appreciation.

Peer-to-peer lending: Participate in peer-to-peer lending platforms that connect borrowers with investors to earn passive income through interest payments on loans.

Nurturing and Scaling Passive Income Streams

Portfolio diversification: Diversify your passive income streams across multiple sources, asset classes, and investment vehicles to reduce risk and maximize potential returns.

Continual optimization: Regularly assess and optimize your passive income strategies, content, investments, and monetization methods to adapt to changing market conditions and audience preferences.

Long-term mindset: Cultivate a long-term perspective and commitment to building sustainable passive income streams, understanding that it may require time, effort, and persistence to achieve significant results.

By creating passive income streams, individuals can generate additional revenue, build wealth, and achieve financial freedom by leveraging their existing assets, skills, and resources to generate income with minimal ongoing effort or active involvement.

CHAPTER 7

Navigating Challenges and Staying Ahead.

Adapting to technological advancements and market trends

Continuous learning: Stay updated on the latest technological advancements, industry trends, and market innovations through online courses, workshops, seminars, and industry publications.

Technology adoption: Embrace new technologies, tools, and platforms that can enhance productivity, efficiency, and competitiveness in your field or industry, such as automation, artificial intelligence, and blockchain.

Flexibility and agility: Maintain a flexible mindset and adaptability to navigate changing market dynamics, consumer preferences, and competitive landscapes effectively.

Overcoming obstacles and setbacks in the digital landscape

Resilience and perseverance: Cultivate resilience and perseverance to overcome challenges, setbacks, and failures encountered in your entrepreneurial journey, viewing them as opportunities for growth and learning.

Problem-solving skills: Develop strong problem-solving skills to address issues, obstacles, and conflicts that arise in your business or career path, seeking creative and innovative solutions to overcome adversity.

Support network: Build a support network of mentors, peers, and advisors who can offer guidance, encouragement, and insights to help you overcome challenges and stay motivated during difficult times.

Continuing education and lifelong learning for sustained success

Lifelong learning mindset: Embrace a mindset of continual growth and improvement by committing to lifelong learning, skill development, and personal development to stay relevant and competitive in the digital age.

Professional development: Invest in ongoing education, training, and certification programs to acquire new skills, expand your knowledge base, and advance your career or business goals.

Networking and collaboration: Engage in networking events, industry conferences, and collaborative projects to connect with like-minded professionals, exchange ideas, and foster meaningful relationships for mutual support and learning.

Future-proofing Your Career or Business

Anticipating trends: Proactively anticipate and prepare for future trends, disruptions, and opportunities in your industry or market by conducting market research, trend analysis, and scenario planning.

Diversification: Diversify your skills, income streams, and business ventures to spread risk, capitalize on emerging opportunities, and adapt to evolving market demands.

Agility and innovation: Foster a culture of agility and innovation within your career or business, encouraging experimentation, adaptation, and continuous improvement to stay ahead of the curve and thrive in a rapidly changing digital landscape.

By navigating challenges and staying ahead in the digital landscape, individuals and businesses can position themselves for sustained success, resilience, and growth amidst uncertainty and disruption, ultimately achieving their goals and aspirations in the digital age.

Conclusion

Embracing the limitless possibilities of the digital age

Reflection: Reflect on the transformative power of the digital age and the myriad opportunities it presents for individuals and businesses to thrive, innovate, and succeed.

Empowerment: Recognize the democratizing nature of the digital economy, which empowers individuals of all backgrounds, locations, and skill sets to participate and excel on a global scale.

Taking action and seizing opportunities for financial growth

Action-oriented mindset: Adopt an action-oriented mindset and commit to taking proactive steps towards realizing your financial goals and aspirations in the digital age.

Seizing opportunities: Embrace a mindset of seizing opportunities, embracing challenges, and pushing past comfort zones to unlock your full potential and achieve financial growth and abundance.

Empowering yourself to thrive in the ever-evolving digital economy

Adaptability: Cultivate adaptability and flexibility to navigate the ever-changing landscape of the digital economy, embracing change as an opportunity for growth and innovation.

Lifelong learning: Commit to lifelong learning, skill development, and personal growth to stay relevant, competitive, and resilient in an increasingly dynamic and interconnected world.

In conclusion, the digital age presents unprecedented opportunities for individuals and businesses to create wealth, fulfill their passions, and make a positive impact on the world. By embracing innovation, seizing opportunities, and empowering themselves through continual learning and growth, individuals can thrive in the ever-evolving digital economy and achieve financial success and fulfillment.

www.ingramcontent.com/pod-product-compliance
Lightning Source LLC
Chambersburg PA
CBHW030100230526
45471CB00003B/1182